'UNITED WE PLAY'

Understanding and Welcoming Our Differences

Illustrated by Ryan Fouracre

Written by Faye Hayden

First Edition

ISBN: 9798683519582

Dedications

From Ryan

To my Mum and Dad, June and Steve Fouracre: Thanks for supporting me and my work over the years as you have helped me overcome every obstacle life threw at me by telling me to keep moving forward and fight for my dreams."

From Faye

To my Mum and Dad, Val and Phil Growcott: the first people to teach me that 'different is not less'.

And to my son Patrick who shows me this every single day.
I love you to infinity and beyond.

Acknowledgments

The Families

We would like to sincerely thank all of the families who agreed to be included in this book. They volunteered their time and images free of charge to ensure we could raise awareness of our differences and to raise vital funds for

Join Our Boys Trust to build a home for Archie, George and Isaac.

The Creators

We would like to sincerely thank everyone involved in creating this book, who gave their time, enthusiasm and expertise free of charge:

Illustrator - Ryan Fouracre

Writer - Faye Hayden –www.facebook.com

/Bedtime-stories-for-mothers-and-others

Editor – Fionnuala Maxwell

Publishing support - Karen Brown

Our Readers

We are **all** educators, educating ourselves and the children in our lives.

We **all** have the power to build an inclusive and accepting society.

By buying this book – you are helping to make that happen.

THANK YOU.

ABOUT JOIN OUR BOYS

George, Issac and Archie Naughton are 3 brothers who live in County Roscommon, which is in the North West of Ireland.

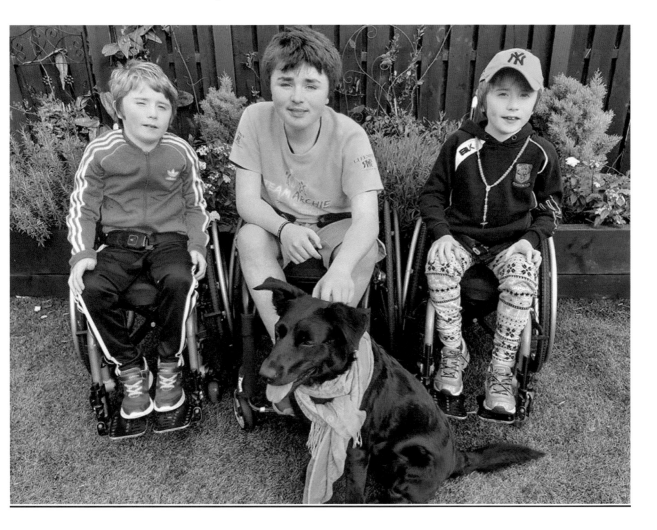

In 2012 their parents, Padraic and Paula received the devastating news that all three of their sons had been diagnosed with Duchenne Muscular Dystrophy. This is a terminal condition with an average life expectancy of 26.

The condition is also debilitating and all three boys are now wheelchair users. The type of wheelchairs they use and the type of equipment they need will continue to change the older they get and the less mobile they become.

Duchenne mainly affects boys, 99% of those diagnosed are male, but girls can carry the gene also. One in every 3500 baby boys are born with the gene worldwide. There are over 250,000 young adults living with the disease all around the world. There is currently no treatment and no cure, but research continues. This disease is catastrophic and the worst nightmare for any parent is that all of their children are diagnosed with it.

Just like everyone else, Archie, George and Isaac have hobbies, hopes and dreams and all three are determined to live their best lives.

You will hear all about George and Isaac in this story, but this is their older brother Archie.

He is 14 years old and in third year at secondary school preparing to take his Junior Cert this year. Archie loves to play basketball and is currently training to be a basketball coach. He also interested in becoming a DJ.

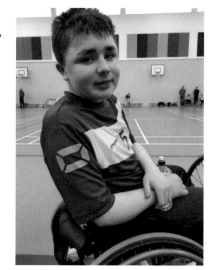

Buying this book means that you are contributing toward the trust fund that was set to:

- build a new home for Archie, George and Isaac to make sure that they have what they need to continue to be able to live comfortably at home together, with their Mum, Dad and dog Sadie.
- contribute to research around Duchenne Muscular Dystrophy in the hope that a cure might be found in time for them.

If you would like to make a donation or find out more about how you can support this cause then please go to:

www.joinourboys.org

Now more than ever, raising funds is very difficult and *anything* you can do to help this family if greatly appreciated.

THANK YOU

About this book

'UNITED WE PLAY' is a book aimed at children to teach them and their parents/teacher about disabilities and how our differences shouldn't divide us.

The book is inspired by the Maya Angelou poem 'Human Family' and is written by Faye Hayden.

The book is illustrated by local Autistic Artist, Ryan Fouracre. is edited by schoolteacher and musician Fionnuala Maxwell and put together by www.coachkarenbown.com

Every child in the book is a real child, living in Ireland (except for Magi who lives in Wales).

The profits from sale of the book will all go to Join Our Boys Trust.

Everyone involved in the book is volunteering their time, effort and enthusiasm free of charge, to make sure as much money as possible is raised for the Join Our Boys Trust.

The aim of this book is to help the family in achieving their goal of raising €400,000 to build a special purpose home for the boys who lose mobility every day.

Please also donate of you can.

More information is available on **www.JoinOurBoys.org**

ERIN

I looked around my classroom and guess what I did see?
Lots and lots of children, who didn't look like me.

How can we look so different, yet all be the same?
I asked myself this question, again and again.

My Mum is very clever and she explained it all to me,
Although we may seem different, we're a human family.

Hi, my name is Erin and I have lots of friends at school,
I like to play with my dolls and go swimming in the pool.

I'm going to introduce you to some people that I know,
We're all the same in many ways, from our head to our toe.

We are also kind of different in our own little way
But one thing that's the same is how we all just love to play.

LUNA

Let's start off with Luna, she's a little smaller than most,
She is from scenic Sligo and lives beside the coast

Luna loves to play at the beach with her big brother Jack.
Gooey Nutella on toast, is Luna's favourite snack.

Luna is smaller because her bones don't grow the same as mine,
They are just a little shorter, but that's absolutely fine.

Luna's great at hide and seek and fits into tiny tight spaces,
But she may not always win at the fast running races.

Luna loves to play with bears and is really smart and funny.
Her smile lights up the classroom making it feel like it is sunny.

Don't forget to ask Luna if she wants to join your game,
Because although Luna may look different, we're all really just the same.

RILEY

Then we have a boy name Riley, you'll see him with his helper dog Willow.
He collects signs that keep us safe, and hides them under his pillow

We cannot see inside his head, but his brain looks the same as mine.
But sometimes it gets wobbly, even though he might seem fine.

Riley is Autistic, and his brain can sometimes feel upset
He might start to flap his hands around, shout out loud and fret.

He just needs some quiet time, to help his brain calm down.
So please don't run away or give Riley a mean or nasty frown.

He'll be back soon to play along or make a painting for the wall,
Riley's really very kind and he will always help you if you fall.

Don't forget to ask Riley if he wants to join your game,
Because, although he may act differently, we're all really just the same

George and Isaac

This is George and Isaac and they are identical twins,
They have really cool wheelchairs, watch them do their spins.

Can you tell which boy is which, it really is a messy muddle.
Both are really friendly and they love to have a cuddle.

They both love playing soccer and like to win the game,
They have a dog called Sadie and she's really very tame.

Their bodies can get tired and need extra time to rest.
But that never stops them being smart and they always do their best.

Isaac is a cheeky monkey and he really loves to read,
George uses a funny voice to ask for what he needs

Don't forget to ask George and Isaac if they want to join your game,
Because although their wheelchairs are different, we're all really just the same.

MAGI

This is lovely Magi, she is really such a cutie
Her favourite flavour ice cream is vanilla tutti-frutti.

She wears a magic machine that is attached to her head.
It helps her hear all the interesting things that I might have said

Magi was born early and gave a scare to her Mum Leah,
And ears weren't quite ready for her to be able to hear.

Magi's best friend is called Isla and they love playing at the park.
She has a dog called Trevor who has the loudest bark!

Magi loves to go for walks and jump in the squishy, squelchy mud,
She loves to hear her wellies hit the ground with a tremendous thud!

Don't forget to ask Magi if she wants to join your game,
Because although her magic machine looks different, we're all really just
the same.

PATRICK

Now here's a boy called Patrick, he's twelve years old.
He loves to play outside, even when it's freezing cold.

Patrick is Autistic, and doesn't feel the world like you or me,
His brain works in a different way, with something called A-D-H-D

It means his brain goes superfast and he finds it hard to be still
And if the teacher says he can't, he shouts I will, I will, I WILL!

Sometimes people think that Patrick is just being silly or bold
But he truly isn't a bad boy, in fact he has a heart of gold.

So, if Patrick is noisy in class some days, and finds it hard to listen
I just remember how much fun he is and that his heart does glisten.

Don't forget to ask Patrick if he wants to join your game,
Because although his brain is different, we're all really just the same

CALUM

Patrick's best friend is called Calum they love making noise,
Teacher says be quiet and shouts, "please just SIT DOWN BOYS!"

Calum is very silly and loves going to watch funny movies,
He eats salty popcorn and drinks strawberry flavoured smoothies

Calum has two sisters, he loves them to the moon and back,
He loves playing Minecraft while eating a chocolate covered snack

Last week in class, Calum tipped over his chair and tried to run away,
Just like his friend Patrick, his brain works in a different way

He has a thing called O.D.D and his brain needs to get everyone's attention
Even if that means he does silly things and ends up in detention!

Don't forget to ask Calum if he wants to join your game,
Because although his brain is different, we're all really just the same

DARAGH

This is Daragh, he is twelve and he soon makes his Confirmation
Sometimes he gets a bit annoyed and shouts out his frustration

Daragh loves it when we eat, and his lunch is always yummy scrummy
He is another child that came out too early from his mummy's tummy

It meant his feet and hands sometimes point a different way
But it never stops him playing soccer every single day.

I love to be on Daragh's team, he really is amazing
He charges at the goal and scores! He does not find it phasing

Daragh needs more time to do his schoolwork with his SNA
But he always finishes in time, to come outside and play

Don't forget to ask Daragh if he wants to join your game
Because although his hands and feet look different, we're all really just the
say

KIRSTY

Now we have my best friend, we all call her Kirsty Boots,
She loves to hang out in the garden, pulling out the plants by their roots.

Teacher sometimes gives out, saying "get the weeds, not the flowers!"
Kirsty looks at her with those big blue eyes, filled with magic powers.

Kirsty does not say a lot, using her machine to tell us what she needs.
If we're doing make and do, she always asks for sparkly beads.

But when I take the time to listen, I know what Kirsty's trying to say,
She likes to pick up leaves in the yard and dance around and play

So, I pick the leaves up with her, and we dance around together
Or we might sit and make a puzzle on the days when it's bad weather.

Don't forget to ask Kirsty if she wants to join your game
Because although her words are different, we're all really just the same.

Matthew

Lastly, we have Matthew he has a lovely laugh,
He loves blowing bubbles, especially in the bath.

We look a little different, because he has one more chromosome than me.
Usually they come in pairs, but Matthew has one set of three!

It's a big strange word that I just do not understand,
I don't really care what it means, we just both like to play with sand.

Matthew loves the water and likes to make a castle moat,
I come along to visit him in my bright blue fishing boat.

Matthew's great at sports and he loves to score a goal,
He gives a big loud cheer and does a celebration roll.

Don't forget to ask Matthew if he wants to play your game,
Because although he looks different, we're all really just the same.

FINALLY

I looked around my classroom and do you know what I did see!
Lots and lots of children, who didn't look like me.

But now I understand that we're all really just the same,
We ALL like to do fun things and to join in with the game.

Our bodies look and work differently in lots of little ways,
But Mum is very clever and I listen to what she says.

That it doesn't matter how we all look, you see
Although we may seem different, we're a human family.

So, us being friends together should not be a hard task,
If you have a question about why we're different - just go ahead and ask!

If someone seems different, remember there is nothing to fear,
Let's all celebrate those differences and let out a booming cheer.

ABOUT THE CHILDREN INCLUDED IN THIS BOOK

Erin

Erin is the storyteller of this book.

Erin is a sibling to a child and has who is Autistic, has Severe Anxiety and ADHD.

Erin has a very close relationship with her big brother Patrick and they love to play together, although they often argue and fallout with each other just like most siblings. Patrick's conditions mean he can get angry when he feels scared and upset – this is often how he communicates just how scared he is feeling.

This can be scary and upsetting for Erin too, but it never stops her loving her brother and she looks after him when he needs her most and forgives him if he has been angry at her, as he never does it on purpose or to be mean.

Siblings to children who need additional support in their life, often don't receive the same amount of attention and time from their parents, who are Carers. They do not complain, and know that's just the way their family works. They too are Carers.

Luna

Luna has Dwarfism. This means that Luna's bones do not grow in the same way as most people and she will be a lot smaller.

People with Dwarfism are often referred to as 'Little People' and will not grow to be above 4feet 10 inches / 145 cms.

Little People can do everything bigger people can do; they just might need to change games a little bit or have a bit of help.

Dwarfism does not affect how clever a person is.

Riley

Riley is Autistic. He does not speak as much as many seven-year olds, but he still has lots to say.

Many Autistic people don't speak or speak differently. There are lots of other ways to communicate though; you just have to look and listen closely.

Not speaking does not mean that the person does not have anything to say or that they cannot hear and understand what is being said to or about them.

Autistic people may have a special interest that they know loads about and love to share with you. Riley's is safety signs, equipment, and London.

Autistic people often keep calm or show their joy by 'stimming'. This can look like hand flapping, rocking, pacing, twirling, screeching or repeating words. It is important never to laugh or ask an Autistic person to stop doing this. It is ok to ask them what they are doing and understand what it means for them.

George and Isaac

George and Isaac are identical twins and they both have a gene in their body that causes them to have Duchenne Muscular Dystrophy like their teenage brother

Archie has this disease too. This means that slowly different parts of their body will stop working the way they used to.

All three boys now use wheelchairs to get around. This means they do things in their lives differently, but it doesn't mean they stop having fun.

There is no cure for Duchenne and the money that you invested in this book will help to build a new home for Archie, George and Isaac that is specially designed to help them keep living a fun life as the way their bodies work changes.

Magi

Magi was born earlier than she was supposed to be and has a severe hearing deficit, which is known as deafness.

Magi has a small machine called a cochlear implant to help her hear. She had to have a little operation to have it. Some of it is inside her ear and some of it is on the side of her head. It has a microphone in it to help her hear. It is important to not touch it if you see one.

Magi has her own book called 'The Monster in the Park' that explains more about her cochlear implant and her life - you can buy the book on Amazon.

Patrick

Patrick is the big brother to Erin our storyteller.

Patrick is Autistic with lots of differences as part of that, he also is diagnosed with ADHD. Many children will have both of these conditions together.

ADHD means Patrick finds it very hard to concentrate or to stay in the same place for very long or in his seat in class or at mealtimes. Patrick moves around a lot and likes to make a lot of noise. Making noise helps him to keep calm and to take in information. It also helps him to concentrate as it blocks out other noises that hurt his brain.

Patrick can often get very upset. He might hit out or say a curse word. This is because his brain gets so confused and goes so fast it is sore inside his head.

Even though Patrick gets upset sometimes, he is really a gentle, kind, caring boy who likes to look after the people in his life.

He gives the best hugs ever and always shares his sweets!

Callum

Calum has a condition called O.D.D. Please don't get confused. This does not mean that Calum is odd! It is just the letters that make up a big fancy name called Oppositional Defiance Disorder.

Sometimes, grown-ups think Calum is being naughty when he does things they don't like. But he isn't. Calum's brain gets very sore and mixed up when he is scared, upset or confused and the only way he knows how to tell people, is with his behaviour. His brain needs caring attention when it feels like this.

Daragh

Daragh has something called cerebral palsy. When Daragh was being born his brain didn't get all of the oxygen that it needed. This means the muscles that make his body work don't work in the same way as most of us, so sometimes his body may move or look a little different.

People with cerebral palsy sometimes use a wheelchair or other equipment to help them. They can do most things everyone else can, just in a different way.

Daragh is a superstar soccer player and he is so good that he has played for Ireland!

Daragh's brain also gets a little bit confused with learning sometimes and may need extra help, so please be patient.

Kirsty

Kirsty has what is called a General Learning Disability. This means her brain doesn't always understand everyday things the way most of us do or it may take her longer to understand. She may find things like household tasks, making friends or understanding her money difficult.

People with a learning disability tend to take longer to learn and may need your help with learning new skills, or understanding complicated stuff.

Kirsty tells us what she needs using a special machine, so be sure to listen to what she is telling you with her machine.

Sometimes if Kirsty doesn't know what is going on and she gets really upset. You can help Kirsty by keeping calm and talking gently too her and getting her something she likes and isn't new to her – Kirsty loves toothbrushes!

Matthew

Matthew has a condition called Down Syndrome.

All of our bodies are made up of things called chromosomes. That is a huge word for something that is actually pretty small. We all have 23 pairs of them, but people with Down Syndrome like Matthew, are super special because one of their pairs is actually a trio.

Children with Down Syndrome often don't hear so well and can find speaking a little bit harder, so you might need to make extra effort to hear what they are telling you.

Often when people with Down Syndrome are young, they use a special kind of sign language. In Ireland this is called Lámh (pronounced lauve like the colour mauve) it means 'hand' but I think it sounds like love.

People with Down Syndrome are filled with love.

Please Support: joinourboys.org
#keep moving #keep marching

Printed in Great Britain
by Amazon